SPIN AROUND THE MALL

The Number of Players: 2–4

The Object of the Game: To exit, or leave, the mall.

The Playing Pieces: One different playing piece for each player; a pencil and a paper clip to use on the spinner.

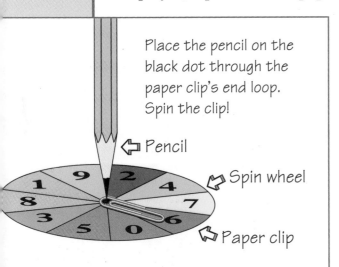

Place the pencil on the black dot through the paper clip's end loop. Spin the clip!

⇦ Pencil

⇦ Spin wheel

⇦ Paper clip

The Play: Players take turns spinning the spinner, adding 10 to the number spun, and moving forward to the nearest number showing that sum. If a player cannot move forward, he or she moves back to the nearest number showing that sum. Two players may occupy the same space.

The Winner: The first player to reach the exit with exactly a 10 or a 19 wins.

Math Concept: Addition with 10.

SEE YOU LATER, ESCALATOR!

MALL MATH

TIME
LIFE *for*
Children ®

ALEXANDRIA, VIRGINIA

I LOVE MATH

Dear Parent,

Who am I? Look for me and some fun toys on page 50.

The *I Love Math* series shows children that math is all around them in everything they do. It can be found at the grocery store, at a soccer game, in the kitchen, at the zoo, even in their own bodies. As you collect this series, each book will fill in another piece of your child's world, showing how math is a natural part of everyday activities.

What Is Math?

Math is much more than manipulating numbers; the goal of math education today is to help children become problem solvers. This means teaching kids to observe the world around them by looking for patterns and relationships, estimating, measuring, comparing, and using reasoning skills. From an early age, children do this naturally. They divide up cookies to share with friends, recognize shapes in pizza, measure how tall they have grown, or match colors and patterns as they dress themselves. Young children love math. But when math only takes the form of abstract formulas on worksheets, children begin to dislike it. The *I Love Math* series is designed to keep math natural and appealing.

I'm looking for the Lost and Found. Can you help me find it on page 20?

How Do Children Learn Math?

Research has shown that children learn best by doing. Therefore, *I Love Math* is a hands-on, interactive learning experience. The math concepts are woven into stories in which entertaining characters invite your child to help them solve math challenges. Activities reinforce the concepts, and parent notes offer ways you and your child can have more fun with this program.

We have worked closely with math educators to include in these books a full range of math skills. As the series progresses, repetition of these skills in different formats will help your child master the basics of mathematical thinking.

What Will You Find in *Mall Math*?

In *Mall Math* your child will discover that math at a shopping mall involves much more than just spending money. There's math in the architecture of the mall, in the people and what they are wearing, and in the places they go—whether it is to buy things, to eat, or to be entertained.

The next time you go to the mall with your child, take the time to do some math: look for angles in the corners of things; see how many outfits you can make by combining articles of clothing in different ways; figure out the time between shows at the movie theater; have your child count the change in your purse or pocket; or estimate how much lunch will cost. We hope your child has fun discovering the variety of math at the mall and will say:

I LOVE MATH!

The Editors
Time-Life for Children

I love playing Three Ball. Can you figure out my score on page 40?

Table of Contents

MIDNIGHT AT THE MALL

It was midnight.

The helicopter landed on the mall roof so quietly that the security guard didn't hear it. He went about his nightly rounds making sure doors were locked and no one was in the mall except the night workers.

Rowena didn't hear the helicopter either. She was busy putting in new light bulbs where the old ones had burned out.

But Ketchup heard it, and she flew through her special window to check out the strange sound on the roof.

MATH FOCUS: GEOMETRY—ANGLES. By looking at pictures of buildings and other objects, children see how acute, right, and obtuse angles are found in the world around them.

Your child can put the tips of both "pointer" fingers together to form an angle. Then he or she can change the size of the angle by moving one or both pointer fingers.

Three small figures climbed out of the helicopter. They seemed worried.

Ketchup landed beside them. "My name's Ketchup. Can I help you?"

"Your name is Ketchup?" asked the red figure. "Maybe you can help us 'catch up' with our lost student!"

"My name is Obtuse Angle," said the widest figure, "and these are my friends, Acute Angle and Right Angle. We teach young angles about making corners."

"All kinds of corners," Acute explained. "Wide ones, like Obtuse, and narrow ones, like me. Squares have corners different from Obtuse and me. Right Angle teaches about those angles."

"Back to our story," said Obtuse. "Late last night, we brought our class to the mall on a field trip to show them how useful angles are. Many of our graduates live here."

"When we got back to our classroom," Acute continued, "Annie Angle, our most curious student, was missing. We had to wait until the mall was quiet again to come back and find her."

"I'll do what I can to help," said Ketchup. "Jump on my back and I'll fly you around the mall."

MORE FUN. Your child can name other objects which, like a ladder, have an angle that changes in size: for example, a pair of scissors.

The minute they entered the mall, they heard voices coming from every corner. Ketchup noticed red lines, green lines, and blue lines outlining corners all over the mall. And the lines were all talking at once.

Hey, Acute Angle! It's good to see you again so soon. Did you forget something?

Annie said she wanted to see more of life than just people's feet so she went upstairs.

We came back to find Annie Angle. Have any of you seen her?

Annie's here somewhere. She's trying to decide whether she'd like to be an obtuse, acute, or right angle when she grows up.

"Let's start the search," said Ketchup. She flew into the arts and crafts shop.

"Look! Annie's been here," cried Acute. "There's her name!"

On they flew to the furniture store. She'd been there, too.

"Oh, no!" the angles moaned. The folding chairs, which were usually stacked neatly along the wall, were unfolded in the middle of the room. Some were open part of the way. Some were open all the way. All the legs of the folding chairs made angles of different kinds!

Suddenly they heard, "Cuckoo, cuckoo, cuckoo," coming from the clock store.

"Why is the cuckoo clock striking three?" asked Right. "It's not three o'clock yet. It's only twenty minutes before one."

They rushed to the clock store, and sure enough, Annie had been there, too! All the clocks were set at different times, so the hands were all at different angles.

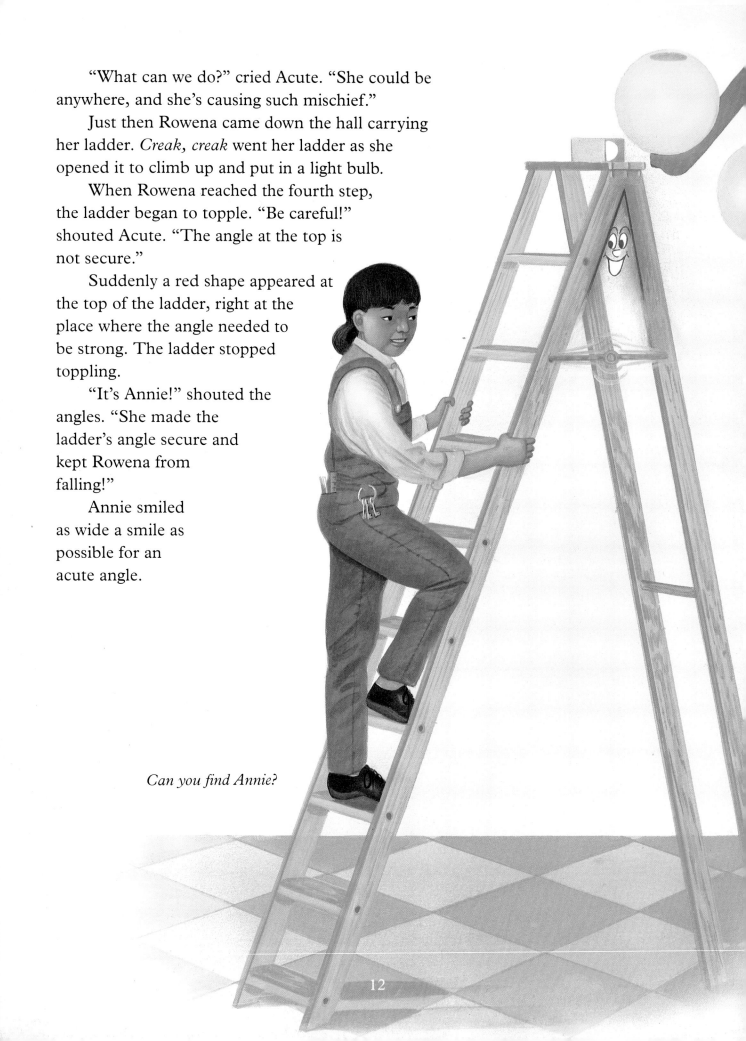

"What can we do?" cried Acute. "She could be anywhere, and she's causing such mischief."

Just then Rowena came down the hall carrying her ladder. *Creak, creak* went her ladder as she opened it to climb up and put in a light bulb.

When Rowena reached the fourth step, the ladder began to topple. "Be careful!" shouted Acute. "The angle at the top is not secure."

Suddenly a red shape appeared at the top of the ladder, right at the place where the angle needed to be strong. The ladder stopped toppling.

"It's Annie!" shouted the angles. "She made the ladder's angle secure and kept Rowena from falling!"

Annie smiled as wide a smile as possible for an acute angle.

Can you find Annie?

"We are glad to see you and proud of you, indeed," said Right. "Thank you for using your wits and keeping the ladder from tumbling. Now it's back to school you go."

Annie climbed on Ketchup's back and said, "Now I know what I want to be when I graduate . . . an angle in a ladder so I can slide back and forth and grow bigger and smaller."

Up on the roof again, Ketchup watched the angles climb into their helicopter and waved good-bye.

"Angles!" she said to herself. "They've been here all the time and I've never noticed them! I wonder how many other things are in the mall that I don't know about. I'll be on the lookout for angles from now on."

Anglebet

Look at the letters around these pages.

B
C
D
E

Can you find letters with acute angles?

Can you find letters with obtuse angles?

F G H I J K

MATH FOCUS: GEOMETRY—ANGLES.
Children explore the angles found in the letters of the alphabet and get hands-on experience by using pipe cleaners to make the letters of their name.

Have available several pipe cleaners or bag twisties.

Z Y X W V

U

T

How many letters can you find
that have right angles?

S

Make
your name.

R

Use pipe cleaners
or bag twisties.

What angles
can you find
in your name?

L M N O P Q

MORE FUN. Help your child find and identify
angles around the house and tell what type each one
is: for example, the corner of a door is a right angle.

Old-Timers & Egg Timers

Just after dawn,
About 6 o'clock,
The old-timers come
To do the mall walk.

They walk and they walk
Down halls or up aisles.
Some measure by minutes,
Some measure by miles.

To measure their pace
Some use an egg timer:
The kind filled with sand,
Or one with a chimer.

How many minutes?
It takes Hazel 4
To walk from the bank
To the jewelry store.

JEWELRY

BAKERY

It takes Mr. Cleveland
From 6:00 to 6:10
To get to the bakery
And then back again.

It takes Mr. Roberts
A minute or so
To walk from a bench
To the art studio.

Elaine Martinez
Sometimes climbs mountains.
It takes her 4 minutes
From fountain to fountain.

MATH FOCUS: TIME—HOUR AND MINUTE.
By solving problems involving minutes and hours,
children become more familiar with elapsed time.

Have your child use a clock or a watch to help him
or her solve these problems. Remind your child that
there are 60 seconds in 1 minute.

When you go to the mall
Next time, take a timer,
A clock, or a stopwatch,
Or one with a chimer.

How long does it take you
To walk store to store?

Does it take you 1 minute,
2, 3, or 4?

Write your times down
And keep a mall chart,
'Cause walking is good
For your legs and your heart.

What a great way
To stay fit and trim,
Using the mall
Instead of a gym.

Mrs. Kowalski
Is quite fast, my friend.
It takes her 5 minutes
To walk end to end.

Benjamin walks
For at least half an hour,
And then he goes home
To take a long shower.

ART
STUDIO

If the mall walkers must finish by 9 o'clock in the morning, how many hours can they spend exercising?

How many minutes does it take Mr. Cleveland to get to the bakery and then back again?

How long would it take Hazel to walk from the bank to the jewelry store and back 2 times?

How long would it take Elaine Martinez to walk between the fountains 5 times?

Use a calculator to find out how many seconds it takes Mrs. Kowalski to walk from one end of the mall to the other.

MORE FUN. Have your child guess and then check how long it takes him or her to walk from the kitchen sink to the front door and then back again.

Caldonia closes her eyes, makes a wish, and throws a coin into the fountain. Plop! It goes down to the bottom of the water.

Uh-oh! That was her special coin, and she's sorry that she threw it into the fountain. Look! It's the guard. He's just about to collect the coins from the fountain to send to charity.

The guard promises to get Caldonia's coin out of the fountain.

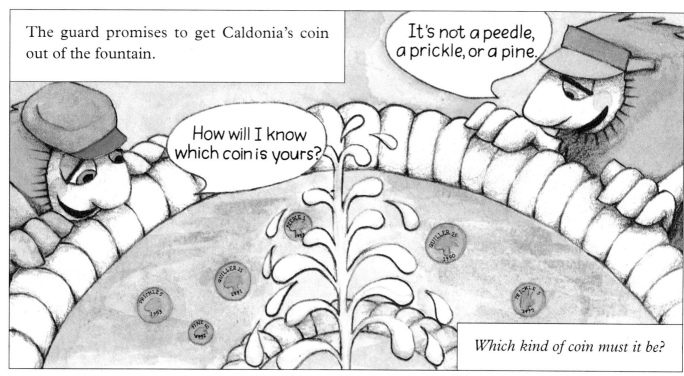

Which kind of coin must it be?

MATH FOCUS: LOGICAL THINKING AND MONEY. Children solve a problem by using the process of elimination. As they compare values of "porcupine coins" with values of U.S. coins, children understand more about money they use.

Tell your child that a peedle has a value of 1, a prickle has a value of 5, a pine has a value of 10, and a quiller has a value of 25. Explain to your child that a number that is the same forwards and backwards (like "1991") is called a palindrome.

The guard pulls out two quillers.

Have a look at these two quillers. Which one is yours?

The date on my special coin is the same forwards and backwards.

Which quiller is Caldonia's, the one on the left or the one on the right?

The guard gives Caldonia her special quiller and she gives him another quiller in exchange.

Thanks for returning my special quiller! Here's another one to replace it.

Thank you! I'll put it in my sack with the other coins for charity.

See if you can answer Caldonia's questions.

What's the date on my *special* quiller?

How many peedles make a prickle?
How many prickles make a pine?
How many prickles make a quiller?

How is porcupine money different from your money? How is it the same?

MORE FUN. Have your child name other numbers that are palindromes: for example, 131, 848, 2992, 67076, and so on.

ANSWERS. The date on the special quiller is 1991; 5 peedles make a prickle; 2 prickles make a pine; 5 prickles make a quiller.

19

MISSING
Lost and Found

Professor Guesser was busy at her desk when the phone rang. "I have a problem," said the voice at the other end. "Did you know that people have stopped losing things? And they have stopped finding things as well," added the caller. "Who are you?" asked Professor Guesser.

"My name is Raymond Schwartz. I'm in charge of the Lost and Found at the mall. No one has turned in anything since the mall was expanded weeks ago. I'm getting lonely, and I'm afraid I'm going to lose my job," he sobbed.

"I'll be right there," Professor Guesser said as she grabbed her helmet.

MATH FOCUS: SPATIAL SENSE AND CHARTS. Children use a chart to help them locate areas on a map.

Help your child use the directory of the mall on page 24 to answer the questions about the locations of the stores.

20

When she arrived at the mall, Professor Guesser couldn't find the Lost and Found anywhere. "That's odd," she thought. "I guess I'll have to ask for help."

She went into the nearest store and asked a salesclerk, "Do you know where the Lost and Found is?"

"No, but I wish I did. Someone left a hat and a pair of mittens on the counter. I'd love to know where to take them."

"Give them to me. I'm sure I'll find the Lost and Found soon," said Professor Guesser. She walked across the hall to ask another clerk for directions. "Do you know where the Lost and Found is?" she asked.

"No, but when you find it, will you please turn in these lost items?" asked the clerk as she handed Professor Guesser a big box.

Professor Guesser went from store to store asking directions. In each store, a clerk handed her something that belonged in the Lost and Found.

What could Professor Guesser use to help her find the Lost and Found?

MORE FUN. Take turns with your child telling the color and number of a store and locating it.

Finally Professor Guesser discovered the Lost and Found behind a potted palm at the farthest corner of the mall.

"These are all for you!" she said.

Raymond Schwartz took the items from the professor and exclaimed, "Lost stuff! I'm in business again!"

Professor Guesser looked curiously at Raymond. "Your problem isn't solved yet. The people who own these items still have to find them, which is next to impossible with the Lost and Found hidden the way it is."

"Really? I never have any trouble," remarked Raymond.

"But you already know where the Lost and Found is," said Professor Guesser. "Shoppers don't. What this mall needs is a map!"

Professor Guesser pulled out her biggest notebook. She made a simple map of the mall, drawing each store as an empty square or rectangle.

Back in her office, Professor Guesser divided the map into 4 sections. Next she colored each section a different color. Then she gave each store in each section a different number. Finally she made a list of the names of the stores. She marked each store's section color, and its number, next to the store's name.

"There!" the professor said to herself. "Shoppers can look for the name of the store they want to visit. Then they can find the section the store is in so they know what part of the mall to go to. Then the store number lets them know exactly where the store is in its section."

MALL DIRECTORY

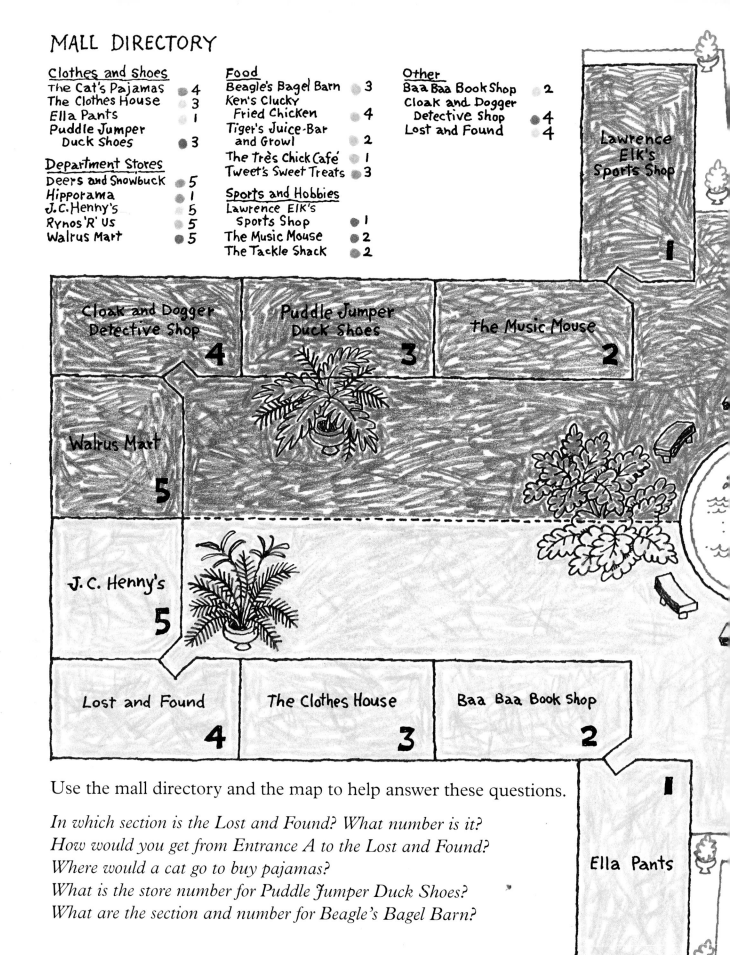

Clothes and shoes
The Cat's Pajamas   4
The Clothes House   3
Ella Pants   1
Puddle Jumper
   Duck Shoes   3

Department Stores
Deers and Snowbuck   5
Hipporama   1
J.C. Henny's   5
Rynos 'R' Us   5
Walrus Mart   5

Food
Beagle's Bagel Barn   3
Ken's Clucky
   Fried Chicken   4
Tiger's Juice-Bar
   and Growl   2
The Très Chick Café   1
Tweet's Sweet Treats   3

Sports and Hobbies
Lawrence Elk's
   Sports Shop   1
The Music Mouse   2
The Tackle Shack   2

Other
Baa Baa Book Shop   2
Cloak and Dogger
   Detective Shop   4
Lost and Found   4

Use the mall directory and the map to help answer these questions.

In which section is the Lost and Found? What number is it?
How would you get from Entrance A to the Lost and Found?
Where would a cat go to buy pajamas?
What is the store number for Puddle Jumper Duck Shoes?
What are the section and number for Beagle's Bagel Barn?

Where would you find The Clothes House?
Where might a hippopotamus go to shop?
Which section is the best one to go to if you're hungry?
Which store do you think is Professor Guesser's favorite?
Where is it on the map?

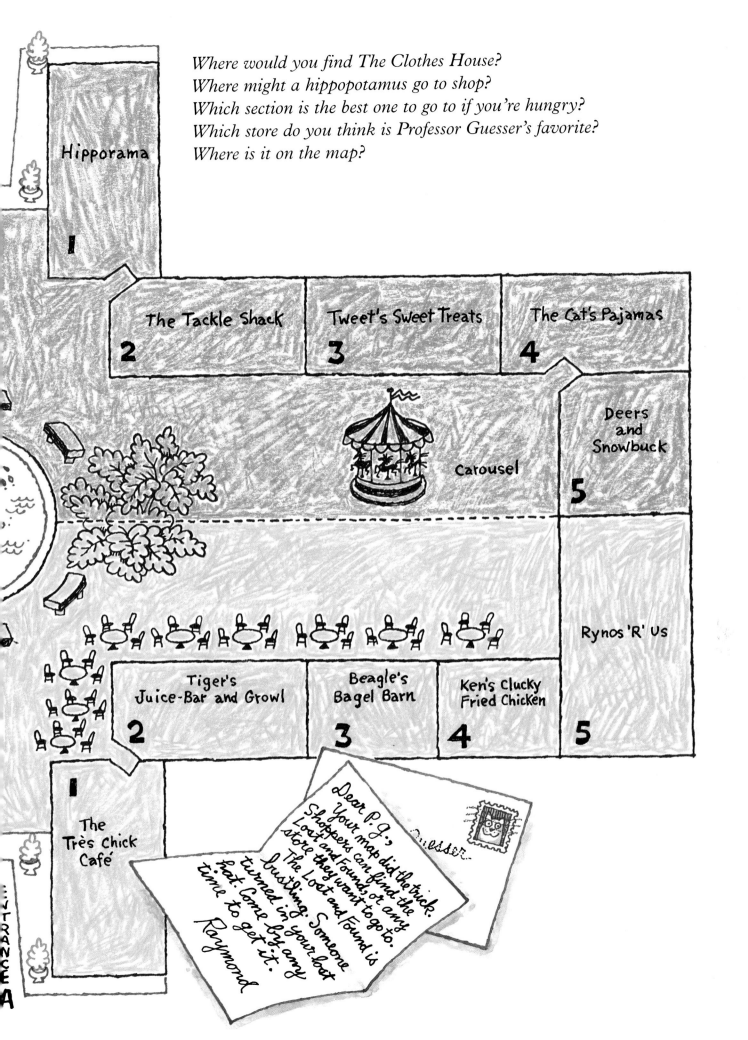

Hipporama

1

The Tackle Shack

2

Tweet's Sweet Treats

3

The Cat's Pajamas

4

Deers
and
Snowbuck

5

Carousel

Rynos 'R' Us

Tiger's
Juice-Bar and Growl

2

Beagle's
Bagel Barn

3

Ken's Clucky
Fried Chicken

4

5

1

The
Très Chick
Café

Dear P.G.,
Your map did the trick.
Shoppers can find the
Lost and Found, or any
store they want to go to.
The Lost and Found is
bustling. Someone
turned in your lost
hat. Come by any
time to get it.
Raymond

Guesser

THE FOOD COURT

JUICE·4·U
SMALL 10¢
MEDIUM 20¢
LARGE 30¢

Buffalo Wings
20¢ each
4 for 75¢

You might think that buffalo wings come from flying buffaloes. But that's not the case! They're actually spicy chicken wings, first served in a restaurant in Buffalo, New York. How much would you pay for 2 wings? How much would you pay for 5 wings?

If you had a quarter and a dime, could you buy a large drink?
If you were buying a medium-sized drink, what coins could you use?
Find the family of 3 sitting at a table. How much do you think they spent on drinks?

MATH FOCUS: ADDITION, SUBTRACTION, MONEY, AND COMBINATIONS. By solving problems, children decide when to add and when to subtract. Have available 4 quarters, 5 dimes, 5 nickels, 10 pennies, paper, and crayons. Tell your child that some of the problems involve adding two different prices: for example, to find the price for 5 buffalo wings, take the special price for 4 wings and add to it the price for 1 wing.

E CREAM SUNDAES
$1.00 for 2 Scoops of Vanilla
with: Hot Fudge
Sprinkles
Butterscotch
Cherries

COOKIES
5¢ each,
2 for 7¢

Wow! A sundae with 3 toppings!
One way you could make your
sundae would be with sprinkles,
cherries, and hot fudge.
What's another way?
Tell more ways you could make a
sundae with 3 toppings.
Draw pictures to help you.

How much would you pay for
3 cookies?
How much change would you get
from a quarter?

MORE FUN. Your child can use crayons and paper
to explore the ways a sundae could be made with
2 toppings.

SNEAKERS

Are your toes breaking through
Your sneakers at the top?
Are they tattered and torn?
Do the soles flip-flop?

Are the laces missing?
Have your sneakers turned gray?
Do they fall off your feet
When you go out to play?

Are your sneakers real stinky?
Do they make you cough?
Does everybody run
When you take your
sneakers off?

Don't look sad.
Don't sing the blues.
Let's go to the mall
To buy some new shoes!

MATH FOCUS: LENGTH. By using a real-life shoe
size chart, children get hands-on measuring
experience.

Help your child use the chart on page 29.

SIZE 2

SIZE 12

SIZE 9

SIZE 5

SIZE 2

Are your feet short and fat?
Are they long and thin?
What size sneakers
Do your feet fit in?

Here's how to find out:

1. Get a piece of paper.
2. Stand on the paper and trace
   (or have someone else trace)
   your left bare foot with a pencil.
3. Cut out the tracing and compare
   your foot to the chart.
4. What size sneakers do you wear?
5. Which pair of sneakers in this
   picture would you buy?

Shoe Sizes

2
1
13
12
11
10
9
8
7
6
5
4
3
2
1

←Place heel of foot here.

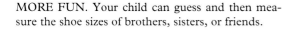

MORE FUN. Your child can guess and then measure the shoe sizes of brothers, sisters, or friends.

Charlie the Chooser

"I want shirts and shorts and hats," said Charlie to his sister, Maria, as they went into the store. "Mom said I could buy 5 things. That means I could buy 1 hat, 2 shirts, and 2 shorts."

"Or you could buy 3 shirts and 2 shorts and not get any hats," said Maria.

"No, I want at least 1 hat. I always wear a hat," Charlie said. "I want to be able to wear lots of different outfits. I wonder how many ways I can combine 1 hat, 1 shirt, and 3 shorts."

"This is a puzzle," said Maria. "Let's eat lunch and figure it out. Then we'll come back and you can buy what you want."

How many outfits do you think Charlie can make with 1 hat, 1 shirt, and 3 shorts?
What other 5 pieces of clothing might Charlie select?

MATH FOCUS: COMBINATIONS. By seeing how different outfits can be formed by putting various articles of clothing together in different combinations, children explore the area of mathematics called Combinations and Permutations.

Help your child follow the arrows in the pictures to identify each clothing combination.

After she finished her sandwich, Maria took paper, a pencil, and some crayons from her pocketbook.

"Here's a picture of a black hat," she said. "You can wear it with a plain shirt. And you can wear the hat and shirt with 3 different shorts."

"I get it," said Charlie. "With those 5 items . . . 1 hat, 1 shirt, and 3 shorts . . . I have 3 outfits!"

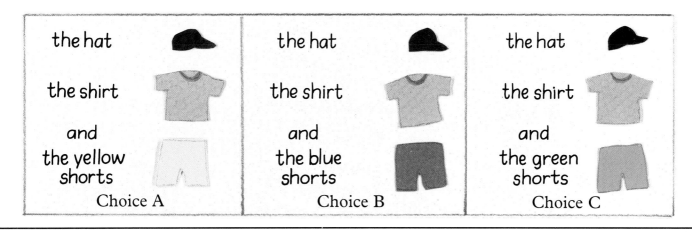

the hat	the hat	the hat
the shirt	the shirt	the shirt
and the yellow shorts	and the blue shorts	and the green shorts
Choice A	Choice B	Choice C

MORE FUN. Your child can select 5 or 6 items of his or her clothing and arrange them in different combinations.

Maria said, "Now let's see how many outfits you can make from 1 hat, 2 shirts, and 2 shorts."

"Here's the hat," she said. "Here are the shirts."

"I see," said Charlie. "I can wear the hat with either shirt."

"And here are the shorts," said Maria. "I'll draw each of them two times."

"You can wear the shorts with the plain shirt, and you can wear the shorts with the striped shirt."

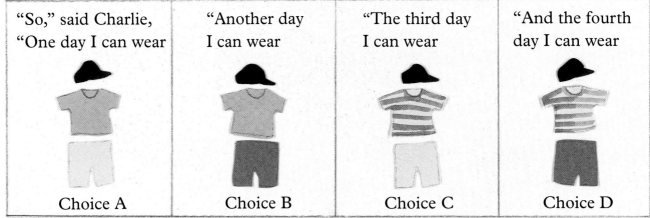

"So," said Charlie, "One day I can wear

Choice A

"Another day I can wear

Choice B

"The third day I can wear

Choice C

"And the fourth day I can wear

Choice D

"FOUR OUTFITS!" shouted Charlie. "I know which 5 items I want to buy!"

The clerk at Kids' Stuff listened while Charlie explained how he chose his 5 items. "You already have a red hat on your head," he said. "How many different outfits could you make if you combined your red hat with your new clothes?"

Charlie closed his eyes for a minute. Then he jumped up and said, "Enough for every day of the week, plus 1, I think! Maria and I will go home and check!"

Here is the chart Charlie and his sister drew.

Remember, Charlie has 6 different items to choose from:

On Monday Charlie wore outfit A. Which clothes did he wear?

On Tuesday Charlie wore outfit B. Which clothes did he wear?

On Wednesday Charlie wore the black hat, the striped shirt, and the yellow shorts. Which letter describes the outfit he wore on Wednesday?

What do you think he wore on Thursday?

For his friend's birthday he wore the red hat, the striped shirt, and the blue shorts. Which letter describes this outfit?

What other outfits could he make?

How many different outfits could he make using these 6 pieces of clothing?

Suppose you had 1 hat, 2 shirts, and 3 shorts. Can you draw a chart to figure out how many combinations of outfits you could make?

THE

Candy

P-Nut Brittle 6¢

Choco-Rolls 1¢

CARAMELS 6¢

SNOW TOPS 5 for 10¢

SOUR BALLS 2 for 6¢

GUM 2¢

CHEW EES

LIFT HERE

LIFT HERE

LIFT HERE

LIFT HERE

LIFT HERE

LIFT HERE

LIFT HERE

You may want to use a calculator to help you answer these questions.

If you had a nickel, what could you buy?

Would it cost more to buy 2 Fire Balls or 2 Sour Balls?

How much would 3 pieces of fudge cost?

MATH FOCUS: MULTIPLICATION AND DIVISION READINESS, ADDITION AND SUBTRACTION, MONEY, AND CLASSIFICATION. Children solve problems by computing with money and using classification skills.

36

Have available 5 dimes, 5 nickels, 10 pennies, and a piece of string about 3 feet long. As an alternative to "lassoing" the candies with string on pages 38 and 39, your child can put pennies on them.

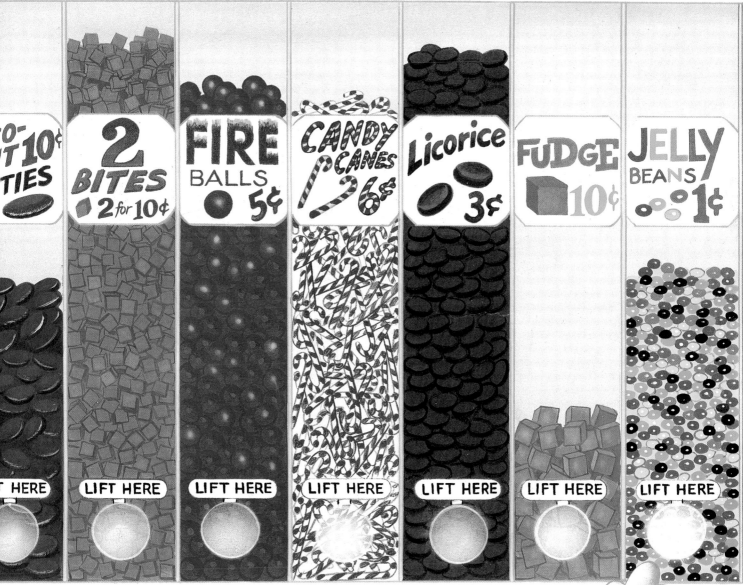

Coral

CO-T 10¢ TIES

2 BITES 2 for 10¢

FIRE BALLS 5¢

CANDY CANES 6¢

Licorice 3¢

FUDGE 10¢

JELLY BEANS 1¢

LIFT HERE — LIFT HERE — LIFT HERE — LIFT HERE — LIFT HERE — LIFT HERE — LIFT HERE

If you had $1.00, could you buy 10 candy canes and 20 Choco-Rolls?

How many Snow Tops could you buy for 20¢?

How many pieces of licorice could you buy for a dime? How much

change would you get?

MORE FUN. Have your child create his or her own
penny-candy word problems and then use coins to
solve them.

I like to lasso things. You can lasso with a piece of string. Try it!

Lasso everything that has red in it.

Lasso everything that is striped.

Lasso everything that has chocolate in it.

Lasso everything that is not striped.

Lasso everything that does not have green in it.

Kyle emptied his bank on the bed and counted the money he had saved to spend at Taco Tiki.

"Kyle, are you ready to go?" called Mom from downstairs.

"Almost. I've got to get my tickets," he called back. Kyle reached up to the shelves of his closet and took down a jar filled with all the tickets he'd saved playing 3 Ball at Taco Tiki. He had been saving for months to get enough tickets to exchange for the prize he wanted. Kyle put the money in his pocket, and carried his jar filled with tickets to the car.

Count the money on Kyle's bed. How much does he have to spend at Taco Tiki?

Look at the jar of tickets. About how many tickets do you think Kyle has saved?

MATH FOCUS: MULTIPLICATION READI-NESS, ADDITION, SUBTRACTION, COUNT-ING, AND GROUPING. By figuring out possible game scores, children practice computation.

Remind your child that one of the possible scores on pages 42 and 43 is zero. Help your child count by tens on page 45.

When they got to Taco Tiki, Kyle's mother ordered lunch and Kyle went over to the token machine. For every dollar bill he fed into the machine, Kyle got back four tokens. The machine also changed each quarter he had for a token.

"Tell me how you play 3 Ball," asked Mom.

"Well," said Kyle, "one token lets me play 1 game. During each game I get to throw three balls. I can score 0, 1, 2, or 3 points with each ball. For each point I score I get 1 ticket."

"That sounds like fun," said Mom.

"I'll be back when the food's ready," said Kyle. Then off he went to play his favorite game.

How many tokens does Kyle have altogether?

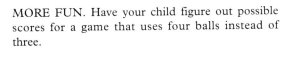

MORE FUN. Have your child figure out possible scores for a game that uses four balls instead of three.

Using all 3 balls, what's the highest score Kyle can get at the end of a game? What's the lowest?

42

Kyle has used all 3 balls. How could he have gotten his score? Tell all the ways you can think of.

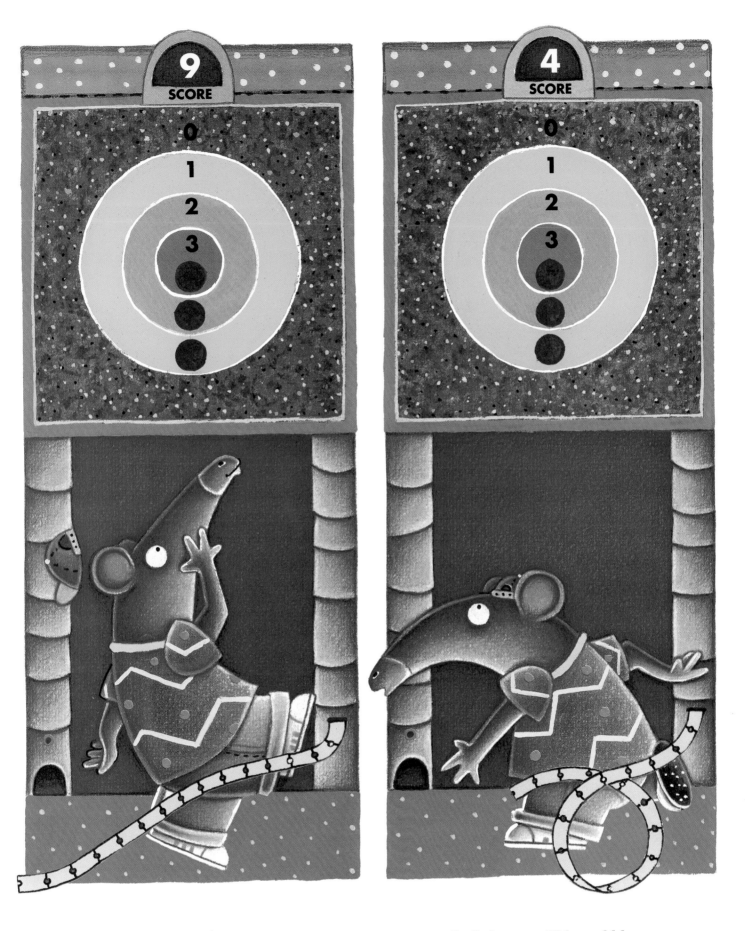

What's Kyle's score at the end of this game? How many ways could he have gotten it?

43

Tell all the ways Kyle could have gotten this score. How many tickets has Kyle gotten so far today?

Kyle had played 8 games by the time lunch was ready.

"What I want costs 100 tickets," said Kyle, clutching a fistful of tickets. "So if I add what I won today to the tickets I saved in my jar, I should have enough. What do you think, Mom?"

"I'll help you count them all after you eat," she said. Kyle quickly ate his Hawaiian Tacos and Banana Fanana Fajitas.

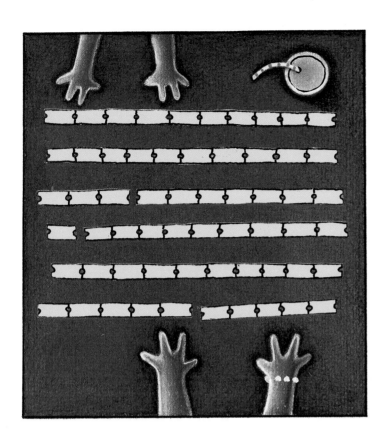

When they were finished eating, Kyle and Mom lined up the tickets from the jar, 10 tickets in each line.

"I sure saved a lot of tickets," said Kyle. "I wonder how many tickets there are altogether."

How many tickets did Kyle have saved in the jar?
How many more does he need to get the prize he wants?

"Let's find out how many tickets you won today," said Mom.

Kyle took the tickets he had won today and lined them up in the same manner. "Wow! I won 45 tickets!"

"That's wonderful, Kyle," said Mom.

"I can save these extra tokens until next time," said Kyle. "Let's go get my prize."

How many tickets does Kyle have in all?
Does he have enough for his prize?
How many tickets will Kyle have left after he gets his prize?

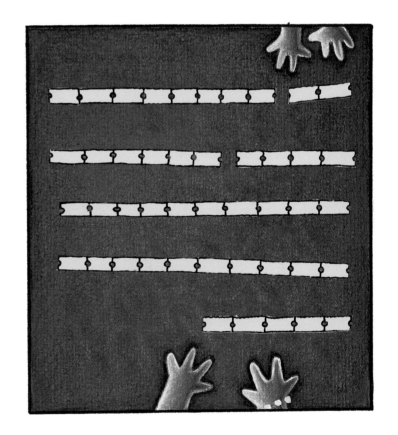

Kyle proudly said to the ticket person, "I have 105 tickets."

"You have lots of choices," she replied. "You can get 2 things that cost 50 tickets, or 4 things that cost 25 tickets, or 10 things that cost 10 tickets. You'll even have some tickets left over."

"But the thing I want costs 100 tickets," said Kyle. "Please give me the prize between the giraffe and the soldiers that is not the ball. I'll put the leftover tickets back in the jar and start saving for my next prize."

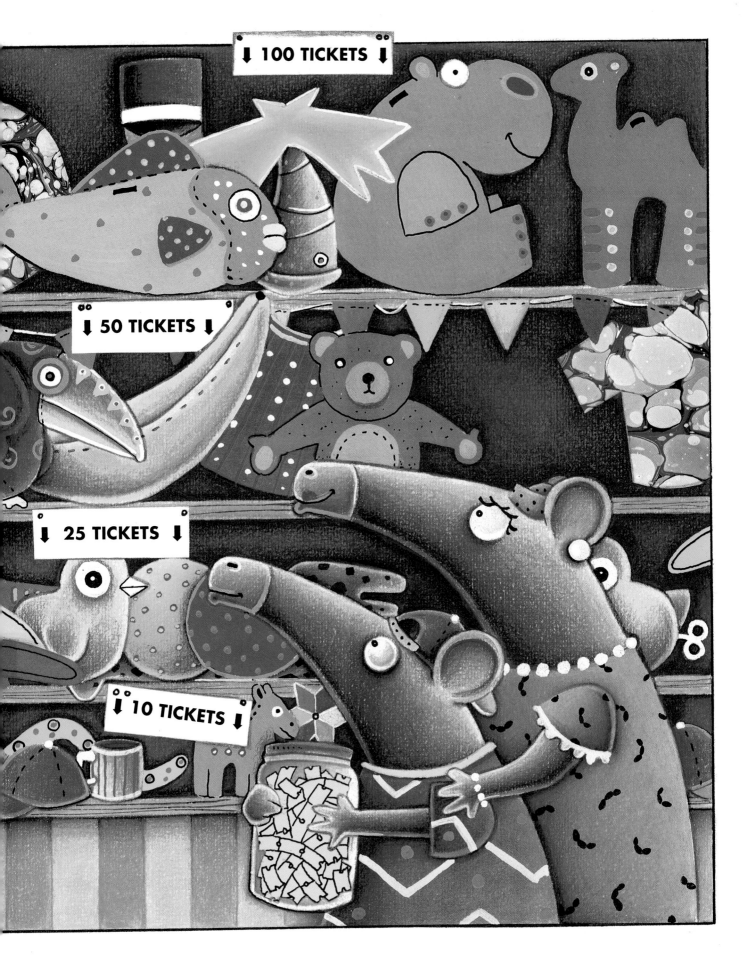

↓ 100 TICKETS ↓

↓ 50 TICKETS ↓

↓ 25 TICKETS ↓

↓ 10 TICKETS ↓

Which prize did Kyle choose?
How many tickets did he have left over?

47

How would you spend 100 tickets?

SEE YOU LATER, ESCALATOR

Tell how the man watering plants can get to the baby shop. Would you send him past the movie theater? Tell how the dog on the skateboard can get to the toy store.

MATH FOCUS: SPATIAL SENSE. By using a picture of a busy mall to solve problems, children develop their sense of the geometric relationships of objects in a given space.

When answering the questions, have your child use directionality terms such as *up*, *down*, *left*, *right*, *next to*, and *between*.

Tell how the woman in the big purple hat can get to the information booth. Then tell how she can get to the sneaker store.

How can the boy eating the huge hot dog get to the post office? The girl with the giraffe is hungry, but she doesn't want pizza. Tell how she can get to the frozen yogurt place.

MORE FUN. Your child can describe a morning at the mall and use the picture to tell how he or she would go from one store to another.

WHO AM I?

MATH FOCUS: LOGICAL THINKING. By solving riddles, children learn to analyze information and to apply reasoning skills.

MORE FUN. Have your child create his or her own riddles about the toys on the shelves and challenge family members to solve them.

I am on the shelf below the shelf with the yo-yo on it.
I am to the right of the robot transformer.
I have a red nose.
Who am I?

I am on the same shelf as the drum.
I have four legs.
I do not have a trunk.
Who am I?

I am on a shelf above the shelf with the frog on it.
I am not on the top shelf.
I am between the football and the truck.
Who am I?

I am on the shelf above the shelf with the truck on it.
I am between the racing car and the bear.
I am not the doll.
Who am I?

I am on the bottom shelf.
I am to the left of the blocks.
I am to the right of the drum.
Who am I?

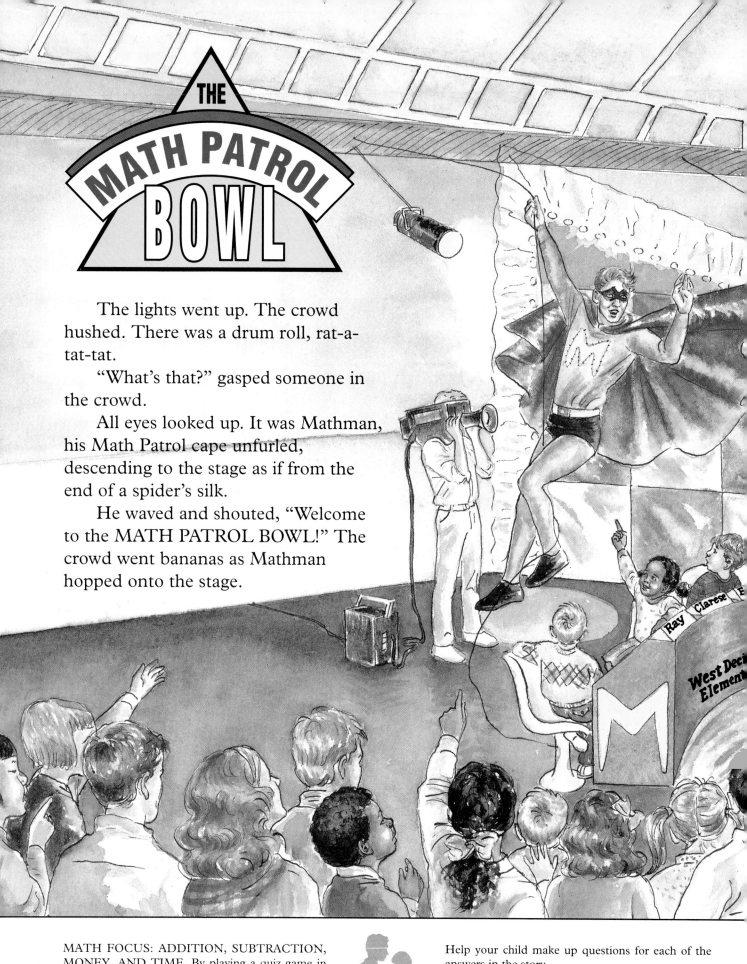

THE MATH PATROL BOWL

The lights went up. The crowd hushed. There was a drum roll, rat-a-tat-tat.

"What's that?" gasped someone in the crowd.

All eyes looked up. It was Mathman, his Math Patrol cape unfurled, descending to the stage as if from the end of a spider's silk.

He waved and shouted, "Welcome to the MATH PATROL BOWL!" The crowd went bananas as Mathman hopped onto the stage.

MATH FOCUS: ADDITION, SUBTRACTION, MONEY, AND TIME. By playing a quiz game in which several different questions have the same answer, children learn to think about things from different points of view.

Help your child make up questions for each of the answers in the story.

"This is the final round of our mall math tournament," he said over the loudspeaker. "Let me introduce our two teams. Team 1 is Ray, Elbert, and Clarese from West Decimal Elementary School. Team 2 is Tommy, Maura, and Iona from Computation Country Day School."

"Go! Go! Go!" chanted the Math Patrol, who were the judges.

"Let's review the rules of our game," said Mathman. "The teams will take turns. I will give an answer. It will be up to each team to ask three correct questions. A team will get 1 point for each correct set of answers. The team with more points wins."

"Here's a practice answer for both teams," said Mathman. "The answer is 5. Team 1?"

Clarese asked quickly, "What is 1 + 1 + 1 + 1 + 1? How many pennies equal a nickel? How many fingers are on one hand?"

"Very good!" Mathman said. "Team 2?"

"Hmm," said Tommy. "What is 6 – 1? How many sides does a pentagon have? How many days a week do we go to school?"

"Excellent!" said Mathman.

"Are you all ready?" Mathman asked the children. They nodded. "Let's begin. Team 1, your first answer is 12."
Elbert raised his hand. "What is 6 + 6? How many inches are in a foot? How many things are in a dozen?"

"Are those questions correct, Math Patrol?" Mathman asked.

"Yes!" they shouted.

Can you think of another question for this answer?

"Team 2, your answer is 9," said Mathman.
"Oooh, oooh, I know," said Iona. "What is 10 – 1? What is 3 + 3 + 3? What is 109 – 100?"

"You are right!" the Math Patrol called out. "Good questions!"

How many other questions can you think of for this answer?

Mathman twirled around and pointed to Team 1. "The answer is Monday." "Elbert, you're the team captain. Quick, think of something," whispered Ray. "Umm," said Elbert. "What day is 2 days before Wednesday? What is the day after Sunday? What is the first school day of the week?"

"Looks like Mathman just can't stump Team 1. They're hot and they're right!" called out the Math Patrol.

What three questions would you give for this answer?

"Think fast, Team 2. The answer is 50¢," said Mathman.

"How much are 2 quarters? How much are 5 dimes? How much would you pay for 10 five-cent candies?" asked Maura.

"Excellent!" said the Math Patrol. Mathman said, "Let's make the answers harder."

Can you think of two more questions for this answer?

57

"Team 1, this is your answer," said Mathman as he pointed to 911.

Ray looked at Elbert and shrugged his shoulders. Elbert shook his head and stared at Clarese. Clarese just rolled her eyes. "That's a very big number," she said.

"I'm sorry," said Mathman. "That's not a question."

"Can we have another number?" asked Clarese.

"That is a question, but it's not a correct question," said the Math Patrol. "Team 2 will have a chance."

"Awwww," moaned the crowd.

Mathman cautioned Team 2, "Remember, if you are correct you will win the tournament."

The crowd hushed. Mathman held his breath. Tommy fidgeted and twirled his fingers. Maura scratched her head.

911

Iona looked blankly at the floor. Then the corners of her mouth began to turn up and her eyes began to twinkle.

"Oooh, oooh, I know," said Iona. "What is 900 + 11? What is 912 − 1?"

"Very good," said Mathman. "One more question and your team wins."

"What is the telephone number you call when there's an emergency?" asked Iona in a loud, clear voice.

"Nine, one, one!" shouted the crowd in unison.

"You're right!" cried the Math Patrol and Mathman together. "That's a great question. Team 2 has 3 points and team 1 has 2 points. Team 2 wins!"

Mathman congratulated each of the contestants as the crowd gave three cheers: "Hip, hip, hooray! Hip, hip, hooray! Hip, hip, hooray!"

And the Question Is...

zero

3 o'clock

100

25

circle

60

MATH FOCUS: ADDITION, SUBTRACTION, PLANE SHAPES, AND TIME. By making up more than one question to a given answer, children use flexible thinking skills.

Encourage your child to be creative when making up questions, and praise all efforts. Keep in mind that there are many correct questions for each answer.

MORE FUN. Take turns with your child saying a mathematical term and making up a question for it.

61

CALCULATOR

WELCOME TO THE MALL MOVIE THEATER!

TICKETS

	AFTERNOON	EVENING
ADULT	$3.00	$5.00
CHILD	$2.00	$4.00

(age 12 and under)

ENTER HERE FOR NEXT SHOW

NOW SHOWING
The Magic Carpet

Matt and Jenny are going to the afternoon show with their parents. How much will tickets for the 4 of them cost?

Meagan, Chelsea, and Christine are going to the afternoon show for Meagan's fourteenth birthday. How much will the girls' tickets cost?

What time does the afternoon show start?

When does the evening show start?

MATH FOCUS: ADDITION, SUBTRACTION, MONEY, AND TIME. By using a calculator to solve problems, children practice adding and subtracting up to four numbers at a time.

For dollar amounts have your child just press the number of dollars and not the decimal point and two zeros: for example, have him or her just press *3* for a price of $3.00. Remind him or her to press the = key to get the answer.

THEATER

NOW SHOWING: THE MAGIC CARPET

Afternoon Show: 3:00 p.m.
Evening Show: 8:00 p.m.

Jim and his father are also going to see *The Magic Carpet*. How much will evening tickets cost them? How much change will Jim's father get from $10.00?

Rachel, Rob, and Chris are going to see the evening show with their mother. How much will Mom spend on the tickets? Mom is going to buy a bucket of popcorn for $2.00. How much will she spend altogether?

Mike's 18-year-old sister Sarah is taking him to the evening show. Whose ticket will cost more? How much more will it cost?

MORE FUN. Your child can make up word problems about ticket prices for your family and challenge others to solve them.

TIME-LIFE for CHILDREN®

Publisher: Robert H. Smith
Associate Publisher and Managing Editor: Neil Kagan
Assistant Managing Editor: Patricia Daniels
Editorial Directors: Jean Burke Crawford, Allan Fallow,
　　Karin Kinney, Sara Mark, Elizabeth Ward
Director of Marketing: Margaret Mooney
Product Managers: Cassandra Ford,
　　Shelley L. Schimkus
Director of Finance: Lisa Peterson
Financial Analyst: Patricia Vanderslice
Administrative Assistant: Barbara A. Jones
Production Manager: Prudence G. Harris
Production: Celia Beattie
Supervisor of Quality Control: James King

Produced by Kirchoff/Wohlberg, Inc.
866 United Nations Plaza
New York, New York 10017

Series Director: Mary Jane Martin
Creative Director: Morris A. Kirchoff
Mathematics Director: Jo Dennis
Designer: Jessica A. Kirchoff
Assistant Designers: Brian Collins, Daniel Moreton,
　　Judith Schwartz
Contributing Writers: Anne M. Miranda, Shereen Rutman,
　　Ellen Sternhell
Managing Editor: Nancy Pernick
Editors: Susan M. Darwin, Beth Grout, David McCoy

Cover Illustration: Don Madden

Illustration Credits: Bob Barner, pp. 30–35; Liz Callen,
pp. 26–27, pp. 62–63; Kathleen Howell, pp. 52–61; Jessica A.
Kirchoff, back end papers; Tom Leonard, pp. 6–13, p. 15,
pp. 36–38; Don Madden, pp. 20–25; Daniel Moreton,
pp. 40–47; Andy San Diego, pp. 18–19; Joe Veno, front end
papers, pp. 16–17, pp. 48–51; Viki Woodworth, pp. 28–29.

Photography Credits: pp. 38–39, Ken Karp, OPC.

First printing. Printed in U.S.A.
Published simultaneously in Canada.

Time Life Inc. is a wholly owned subsidiary of THE TIME INC.
BOOK COMPANY

TIME-LIFE is a trademark of Time Warner Inc. U.S.A.

For subscription information, call 1-800-621-7026.

CONSULTANTS

Mary Jane Martin spent 17 years working in elementary
school classrooms as a teacher and reading consultant; for
seven of those years she was a first-grade teacher. The
second half of her career has been devoted to publishing.
During this time she has helped create and produce a wide
variety of innovative elementary programs, including two
mathematics textbook series.

Jo Dennis has worked as a teacher and math consultant
in England, Australia, and the United States for more than
20 years. Most recently, she has helped develop and write
several mathematics textbooks for kindergarten, first grade,
and second grade.

Catherine Motz Peterson is a curriculum specialist
who spent five years developing an early elementary
mathematics program for the nationally acclaimed Fairfax
County Public Schools in Virginia. She is also mathematics
consultant to the University Of Maryland, Catholic
University, and the Fredrick County Public Schools in
Maryland. Ms. Peterson is the director of the Capitol Hill
Day School in Washington, D.C.

Dr. Helene Joy Silverman is a professor of early
childhood and elementary education at Herbert H.
Lehman College, City University of New York, and a
co-director of the New York City Mathematics Project.
Following service as a teacher in the New York City
public schools, she became an author of children's
materials, a contributor to several math textbook series,
and a math consultant to many school districts.

Library of Congress Cataloging-in-Publication Data
See you later, escalator: mall math.
　　　　　p.　cm. —— (I love math)
　　　　Summary: Stories, poems, riddles, games, and
hands-on activities introduce early math skills, focusing
on the mathematics one might encounter on a trip to the
shopping mall.
　　　　ISBN 0-8094-9974-6
　　　　1. Mathematics—Juvenile literature. [1.
Mathematics. 2. Mathematical recreations.] I. Time-
Life for Children (Firm) II. Series.
QA40.5.S44　　1993
513 — dc20　　　　　　　　　93-6494
　　　　　　　　　　　　　　　CIP
　　　　　　　　　　　　　　　AC

The Number of Players: 2-4

The Object of the Game: To score the highest number of points after flicking 5 pennies onto the game board.

The Playing Pieces: 5 pennies for each player; pencil and paper for scoring.

The Play: The first player places 5 pennies on the starting line and flicks them onto the game board with his or her index finger. The player uses all 5 pennies and then adds up his or her score before another player begins. If a penny lands on a line, the player takes the score from the scoring area where most of the penny is. If the penny is halfway between 2 scoring areas, the player takes the greater score. If a penny is off the board, the score for that penny is 0. When everyone has had a turn, the game is over.

The Winner: The player with the highest score wins.

Math Concepts: Addition of several numbers.
Counting by 10's.
Spatial relationships and geometry.